A Broken Vow:
My Story from Virgin to Single Mother in 4 Months

Jasmine Henderson

Copyright © 2013 Jasmine Henderson. All rights reserved.

Edited by Kimberly McGuire

Photos by Angelina Legaspi

Scripture quotation taken from *The Hebrew-Greek Key Word Study Bible* - King James Version
Copyright © 1984, 1991 by AMG International, Inc. All rights reserved.

ISBN: 1494764520
ISBN-13: 978-1494764524

DEDICATION

To God, my faithful and true Redeemer

To Paul, my beautiful and precious gift

To my family, my ever loving support

CONTENTS

	Acknowledgments	i
	Preface	iii
1	Peeing On a Stick	1
2	Telling Family	6
3	Rejection and Reality	13
4	How Did I Get Here?	26
5	People's Judgment and God's Forgiveness	36
6	Finding My Pearls	45
7	My Truth About Sex and a New Resolve	51
	What's Your Story: Starting the Conversation	57

ACKNOWLEDGMENTS

Thank you, God, for allowing me to give You honor and praise through the gift of writing You have given me.

Thank you, Mom and Dad, for your open arms and laughter! I am endlessly grateful for your love, wisdom, and friendship. I'm the mother I am because of you.

Thank you, my amazing family, for always believing in me and for the countless hours of babysitting.

Thank you, Faith Tabernacle Church, for all of your unconditional love and support and providing the perfect church home for my family.

And to my LP109 family, my Captain, Joseph, and coaches, Nicole and Abram, thank you for being in the trenches with me, fighting for my dreams as though they were your own. I'm soaring!

PREFACE

There's a lot of education, publicity, and entertainment about teenagers becoming pregnant, but no one ever talks about what happens after high school. Finding out you have an unplanned pregnancy at any age is still shocking, still life-changing. Sure, maybe you're not a "kid" anymore, but there are still consequences, both good and bad, that you carry with you for the rest of your life.

As a young woman committed to abstinence, living in Los Angeles, I never found anyone having conversations that would help encourage me to stay pure. It seemed that the older I got, the more entertainment, books, and the general public just assumed I had either already gotten married or already started having sex. In writing this book, I intend to end this silence, start real conversations, and share the realities that were my situation and may be yours right now or someday will become your own.

So here's my story of when I was 25 and pregnant.

JASMINE HENDERSON

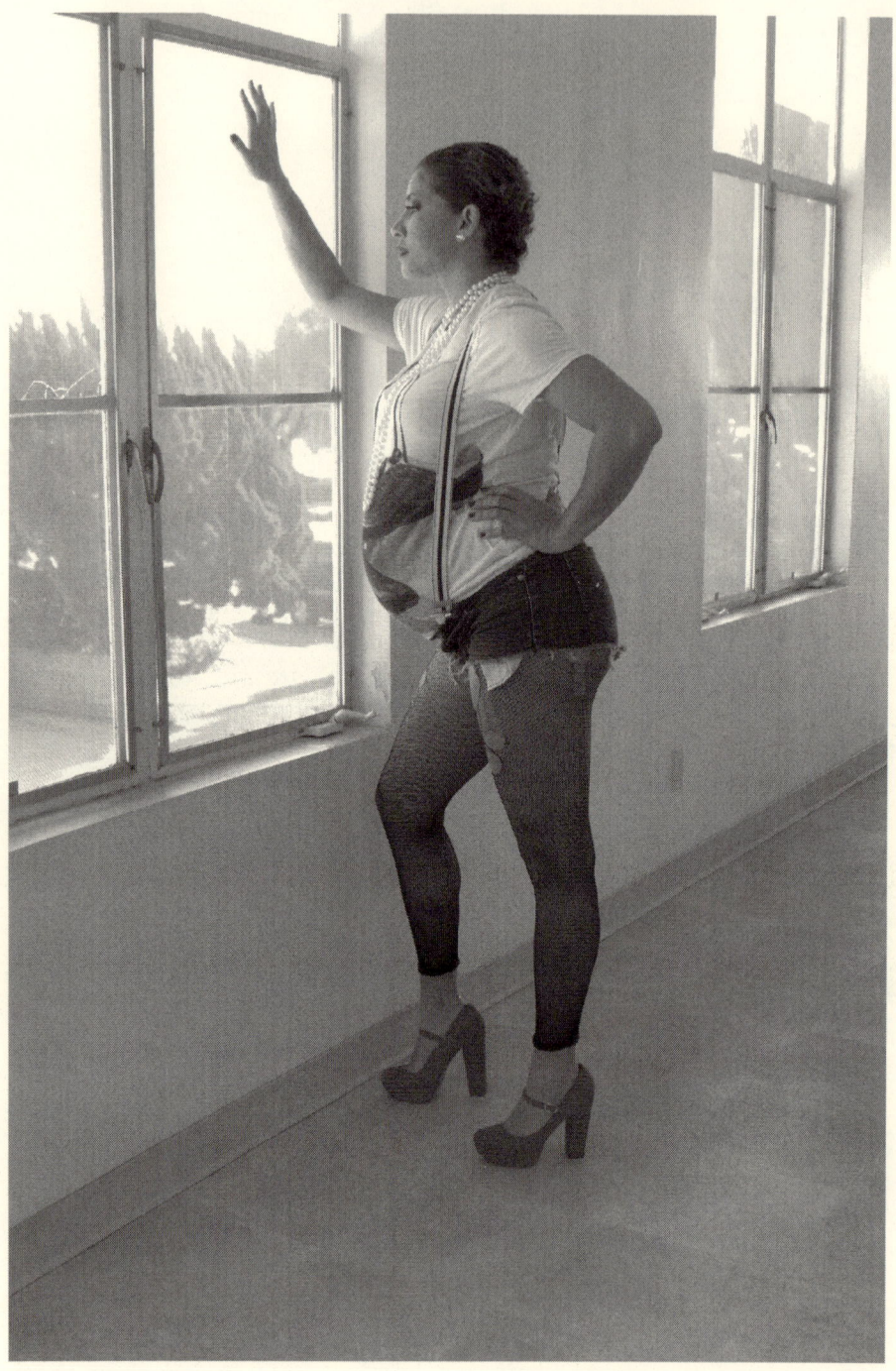

1 PEEING ON A STICK

To set the scene, my pregnancy was nothing more than miraculous in my mind. One could call it "dumb luck," but I know that it was purposed for my son to be on this earth. I was abstinent for twenty-five years and was only sexually active for a month and a half when I got pregnant. I thought I had timed my cycled, but it was one time we didn't use protection. Days later, I even took a morning after pill and had what I thought was a period a week later. To be honest, I had even drunk alcohol while on a trip with my ex and his parents. And really, with what seemed like everyone being sexually active and downright promiscuous, what were the odds that my first time out and around the block would end up with such a costly price?

You see, my boyfriend and I were already broken up for almost a month by the time I had truly suspected I was pregnant. In fact, I had a try-out for the WWE, World Wrestling Entertainment, in Florida less than two weeks away. My flight and hotel were booked and paid for, my itinerary received, and my confirmation made. The possibility of a whole new life was lying before me. I thought to myself: *Maybe this is why he and I had broken up.* I believe that things happen for a reason, and at the time, I thought this was it. I even felt comfortable enough to tell my ex of my new plans, feeling like I could have some closure and move on.

To make sure I was as fit as possible, I was working out every day and weighing myself as well. The suspicion came when instead of losing weight, I had gained a pound, and two days later, I gained yet another pound. It finally hit me that there was a chance I could've been pregnant. Before that, yeah my stomach was a little spotty, but I wasn't throwing up and just thought it was the readjusted diet I had put myself back on. Sure my boobs were a little bigger, but I was assuming that was just because my period was around the corner. And what about that ever telling period? Ok, it had been a while since it graced me with its presence, but I just chalked it up to the morning-after pill I had taken. I had another "period" only a week after having my usual one…*maybe it had thrown off my hormones.* Call me crazy for not putting it together sooner, but being a trained and professional athlete, the weight gain was the proof that maybe the other things weren't just coincidences.

Then the questions came. *Should I just focus on my try-out in Florida and deal with the possibility when I come back? What if they like me and choose to sign me and I am pregnant? If I am pregnant, might I be body slamming my baby every day in training?* The last question was what forced me to face the test. Could I really live with the fact that I could harm my potential baby just because I was selfish and wanted my chance, no matter what the cost? So it was time to head to the drugstore.

At this point, only my two sisters and a friend even knew that I had become sexually active with my boyfriend. So I told my younger sister of my fear. She went with me to buy a pregnancy test, and we were going to pee on sticks together. I appreciated the sisterly support, but I was still scared to death. I had never in my life had to worry about being in this situation before, and I, quite frankly, was embarrassed to have to purchase such a product. When we got to the section of the store, I could feel my cheeks fill with color. *Which one to choose?* After reading and pricing all of them, I finally purchased a box.

There we were. The moment of truth. We read the directions, and I went first. *Did I do it wrong?* Right away the second line had popped up. I looked at the stick, and then looked at the box. *Maybe it's because I missed and hit the middle of the stick where the sign was and not just the end tip. Surely it shouldn't show up so quickly.* My sister did hers, and after waiting the allotted time, her test came up negative. Well, we had only bought the box of two. So I went to bed in disbelief, still thinking of the possibilities of my potential pregnancy.

The next morning I woke up super early and headed back to the drug store by myself to buy one more test. I was determined to know without a doubt in my mind. When I returned home, I headed straight to the bathroom, ripped open the box, and made sure there were no hiccups this time. Only seconds from conducting the test, still in my hands, that second line popped up again, and it hit me. *I'm pregnant.* Fear and the shocking realization filled my mind, and tears flooded my eyes. I walked downstairs and cried for about half an hour straight. Finally, I woke up my sister to tell her the news. I could tell my tears and expression scared her by the look and reaction on her face. "Dawny, I'm pregnant," I said through my tears trying to catch my breath. "What am I going to do? How am I going to tell Mom?"

A BROKEN VOW

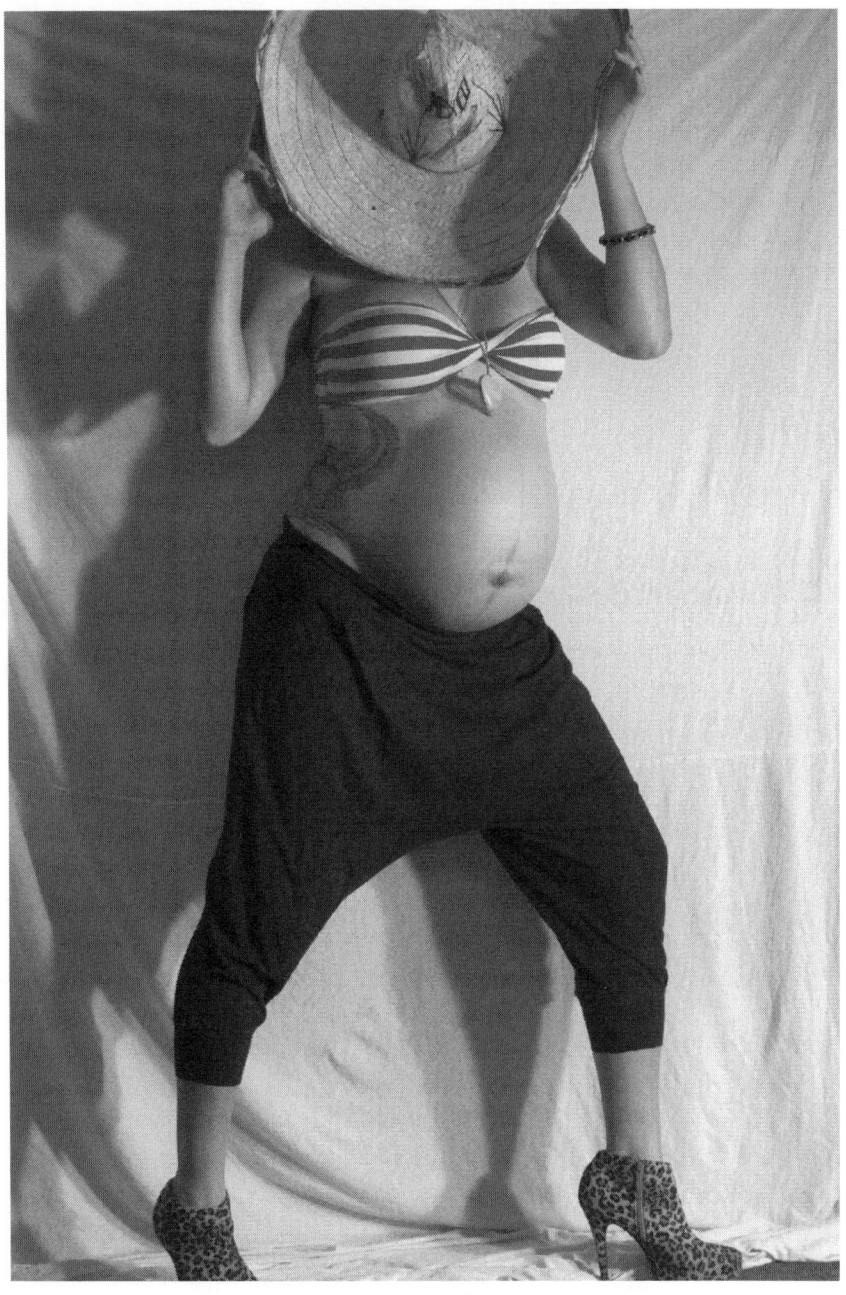

2 TELLING FAMILY

Telling my family was the hardest, most painful, and worst thing I had to do, even worse than telling my ex-boyfriend. I dreaded the possibility of seeing disappointed looks on their faces which seemed inevitable, and I felt guilt and shame even before they could open their mouths to say anything or react. You see, I was the "good girl" of my immediate family. I always got good grades, always went to church, always excelled in sports, and always placed myself in leadership roles such as class president or captain. I was the only one out of five kids who had stayed committed to being abstinent. I was the last one anyone thought was going to get pregnant out of wedlock. But family is family, and my family is so close that telling them wasn't even a question.

MOM:

My first thought was that I had to tell my mom, but what was I going to say? I'd been a virgin all my life. It was only with this recent relationship that I had decided I wanted to have sex. It had never been a problem before. Sure I questioned it, and we even had discussions. But I never faltered from my commitment to stay abstinent. *Great! Now, not only do I have to tell her that I'm no longer a virgin but that I'm pregnant. What is she going to say? Can I bear her disappointment?*

No matter what fears I had, I knew I had to tell her and tell her right away. At the time, my mom and I worked at the same school, and I still had about an hour and a half before I needed to clock in for work. I immediately drove down to the school. She was in the front office as usual, and I asked if I could speak with her in private. I knew she could tell by the redness of my eyes and insistence on speaking privately that something major was wrong, but I don't think anything could've prepared my mom for the moment we were about to share.

Once we finally made our way through the school to the private room, I burst into tears again. Not knowing how to say it, I just did, "Mom, I'm pregnant." A look of disbelief was written all over her face, and as I continued to sob, I saw that she was crying now too. After crying together for a while, I said, "I'm so sorry, Mom." She said that she wasn't crying because she was disappointed in me but because she knew what it meant for me. She knew how dramatically it would change my life, how my dreams and goals would be decisively harder to achieve. Life would forever be different.

We called the doctor to make an appointment to officially be told whether I was pregnant or not. Next, we went through the details on whose child it was and how I was going to tell everyone else. I had to explain to her that my ex was the only one, my only one. And after, there-in lied the million dollar question: How was I going to tell everyone else?

SISTER #2:

Well, my younger sister already knew from the beginning, but my older sister, who also worked at the school, had yet to find out. But once I told my mom, it wasn't long that my sister found out. I obviously had to miss work that day so I could go to the doctor's appointment, and my mom told her what was going on. Her reaction was shock of course, but when I saw her in person, she told me how much she loved me and how I had her full support.

BROTHER #1:

I have two older brothers, one that is six years my senior and another who is only a year and a half. My brother who is closest to me in age is also the one I am closer to. He and I use to be fierce competitors with each other when we were kids, but as we got older, that competitiveness amongst ourselves turned into fierce support for the other to follow their dreams. We've talked and planned about the future, giving each other advice on relationships, encouragement to achieve our highest goals, and suggestions on strategies and ways to get there. As my mom had told me, this would change everything. Now I had to tell and explain to my brother why I wasn't going to Florida.

My brother at the time was going to golf college in Temecula. Friday morning was the day that everything went down, from the second stick test to telling my mom. So why not have it be the day I tell my brother as well? It just so happened that he was coming home for the weekend, and by the time I had come back from the doctor's office, he was already home. I walked in the door, eyes still bloodshot and puffy, when I saw him come to meet us in the kitchen. I started crying all over again, and my brother, naturally, asked what was wrong. I could see he was holding his breath with a look of expecting to hear the worst. The worst being that I had hurt my knee again, preventing me from going to the try-out. Well, I did have something that was going to prevent me from going to the try-out, but an injury would have nothing to do with it. When I told him, he stood there absolutely speechless for what seemed like forever. He eventually snapped out of it and asked questions and expressed his concern and support, but I could tell that he was still in shock and stayed in that state for quite some time.

DAD:

I was petrified to tell my dad. I was his "little bruiser" who always did right and did what she was supposed to do. Surely I wasn't going to end up in a situation like this. At first I felt like it was a cop-out when my mom and I decided that she would be the one to tell my dad, but looking back on it, I'm really glad and thankful that she did. Apparently, from what I gather, my dad was more than livid. His heart was hurt.

It must have been God because the next day he got pretty sick and stayed in his room for most of the weekend. He said he was really glad that he had that time to himself because it gave God time to work on his heart. By the end of the weekend, my dad came out and gave me a hug. He said that it had been revealed to him (God had reminded him) that all things work together for the good of those who follow the Lord. My baby would be a blessing even though it came out of bad decision making. It felt really good and relieving to hear my dad say that and still show me love.

GRANDMA:

Another person I really didn't want to tell face to face was my Grandma. I had no idea how she would react, but I couldn't bear the thought of her always loving eyes filled with disappointment.

My grandparents got married when they were young. My grandma was eighteen and my grandfather was twenty-five, and they remained together for over fifty years. My grandfather passed away when I was twenty-one. He was a pastor and helped found a Christian school with my grandma. I was raised in that church and school. It was where I was working at the time. My grandma was the only grandparent I had left, on either side. She represented what was left of the spiritual backbone I had been raised with. And now I had to tell her, again, that I was no longer a virgin and that I was pregnant. I couldn't bear the thought. My mom already had a feeling I was too scared, too ashamed to tell her and so took on telling my grandma herself. The reaction was one I never would have imagined.

When my mom came back from telling my grandma, I was waiting anxiously to see how she'd taken it. If anything, she responded the most positively saying, "Oh, what a blessing!" She later told me how my grandpa was looking down on me and smiling. I should have expected nothing less…my grandma showing me absolute love.

You could imagine that this was a lot of news to go over with key people over the few days that make up a weekend, and I still had more family to tell. But no one would be as key to tell as my baby's father.

JASMINE HENDERSON

3 REJECTION AND REALITY

That weekend was possibly the longest weekend of my life, but the hardest part wasn't even over. Now I had to tell my baby's father. I mulled over it on Monday and Tuesday. I went from being so sure in telling him to thinking maybe I shouldn't. I know my mom meant well, but the more I spoke with her about it, the more scared I got about all the possibilities, all the unknowns of what he could or would do. *Is he gonna want it? What if my baby has to go from one house to another? What if he tells his parents? Are they going to want us to get married? I don't want to marry him. What if he doesn't want to take care of my baby, but they force him to? Will I have to deal with custody battles and visitation rights and end up dealing with him and fighting with him for the rest of my life? Will he become a dead-beat dad, in and out of my child's life, unpredictable and unreliable? He was too immature to even handle a relationship...can he handle being a father? Should I even tell him?*

All these thoughts were racing through my mind, and I had to decide if I was going to tell him or not. Finally, I had come to the conclusion that, for the sake of my baby, I would tell him. I came to the mindset and realization that I wanted to be above reproach when it came to my child. I couldn't live with the idea of my baby growing up one day and asking me about his father and resenting me for not even giving him a chance. *What if he was a great dad? What if everything turned out just fine?* The truth is I didn't know what was going to happen, but I owed my baby at least the chance of having his father in his life. It was time to choose responsibility yet again. I had gotten myself into this mess, and indeed, it could turn out messy. But I had created it so I needed to deal with it.

So I had made my decision to tell him I was pregnant but didn't know when or how I was going to. Leave it to social media to be the catalyst.

On Tuesday, a Facebook notification popped up on my phone. It was an invitation from him to his birthday party that Thursday night. *Oh, my gosh, his birthday!* In all the dramatics, I had forgotten about his birthday. We had been broken up for about a month and had only one conversation since then. The invitation, I have to admit, gave me a little hope because the "reason" we had broken up was because he had expressed that he wanted to date casually, and I told him that I didn't become his girlfriend so we could date "casually." And even after we broke up, he had texted my mom to tell her happy mother's day. So in my mind for a split second, I was wondering whether there was a slight chance that we could in fact work things out. I looked on the invitation page to see whether I had been selected or just mass-invited because for a moment, I entertained the idea of just going to the party and seeing how things went between us. This thought was just for a moment (haha)! What was I going to do…reveal I was pregnant in a club? Ta-da! Happy Birthday, you're a father! No! I quickly came down from that thought, but the reality remained. I was going to have to tell him, and I was going to have to tell him soon.

I decided on Wednesday that I would call him, not only because it was his birthday party on Thursday night but because my first OBGYN doctor's appointment was that Friday. I wanted to give him the opportunity to go with me if he wanted to.

I prayed and prayed. *Lord, whatever he decides, may it be either fully in or fully out.* I couldn't stand the thought of a dead-beat dad or absentee father. I just wanted black or white…committed or not. I practiced exactly what I was going to say as my heart pounded in my chest and warmth flushed my face. I was in a room all by myself at work mid-morning when I called. He picked up with the same easy-going, flirty greeting, and I knew I had a difficult task ahead of me. I told him that I didn't know how else to ease into it. "I'm pregnant," I flat out said to him. I told him that he didn't need to say anything at the moment but could call me back when he was ready to talk about it. I had figured that since I had time to process it, he should have the time as well. But he didn't take the time. Immediately he retorted, "Are you sure it's mine? Have you had sex with anyone since me?" At this, I was insulted and hurt, not only because I was being questioned about the integrity of my statement but more importantly because by him asking me about sleeping with someone else, it was clear that he had. Any illusions I had about he and I sharing something special were just that…illusions. I explained to him that I had not had sex with anyone else. "Are you going to get an abortion?" I couldn't believe the words actually came out of his mouth. I told him I wasn't. "You know I don't believe in abortion," I told him. He knew I was supposed to be going to Florida for my try-out. "So what about Florida?" I told him that my plans had changed. He was clearly freaking out, and I reminded him about my invitation to take time to think about it and process it. But he didn't want to call me back, actually, instead he spent the next five minutes trying to convince me to have an abortion.

After standing my ground over and over, I finally interrupted him. "You know, I just wanted to tell you now in case you wanted to come with me on Friday to the doctor." I proceeded to tell him that in this appointment I would get to see how far along I was and if everything was working fine. I learned from my older sister that the first trimester is the most tumultuous one, and you're at the highest risk for a miscarriage. After I explained this to him, I could feel him take a breath, and he went from not wanting to have anything to do with it to wanting to call me after the appointment. I got defensive. "Why are you going to call me?" It quickly came to mind that he only wanted to call me to see if I was going to miscarriage or not. *Thanks for caring.*

The conversation was over, and I began to cry. I knew I had prayed for him to either be in or out, but I definitely wasn't expecting him to choose out and, worse, choose abortion. We went to church together; we went to mass together. I felt rejected and cast aside all over again. When I came downstairs to explain to my mom and sister how it went, it hit me even more. My mom tried to rally my spirits by saying it was a good thing, a less complicated thing, and she was right. But it didn't make hearing it any less hurtful. To be honest, I felt unvalued and unwanted. I wasn't expecting him to be that selfish. I thought that there was at least some feeling he had for me that would muster up the sense of responsibility. But all he wanted to do was run away. "I wish you hadn't told me," is what he said in the end. If he had it his way, he would like it to be as if it never happened, and that's how it remains to this day for him.

But something magical happened when I went to the doctor's that Friday. When they did the ultrasound and I saw my baby for the first time, tears filled my eyes and a sensation washed over me. I was over joyed, and I was going to protect my baby whatever the cost. Nothing else in the world mattered. I saw its little head, body, feet and hands. It was dancing and moving the moment we saw it up on the screen. I was almost three months pregnant. This child was mine.

My ex didn't call Friday, but he did Saturday. I was strong for my baby. I had already decided that he wasn't going to steal my joy and that anything he said from this point on wouldn't phase me, but in the end, it did. I was talking on the phone in full excitement, subconsciously maybe trying to get him to feel the same, yet even after I had explained what I saw on the ultrasound and that I was almost three months in, it didn't matter. He still asked me about abortion! I stayed some-what calm as I defended my baby, but inside, I was irate. "You're not killing a person," he said. *Seriously?* It has a head, body, feet and hands. Its little heart is beating. It was dancing for goodness sake! I told him all this, and he didn't care, too selfish to care, too full of himself to care. From that moment on, I knew how to act, and I let him know everything that was on my mind. I asked health questions to satisfy my doctor's request, and finishing up the conversation, I served him reality. I told him that I would not pursue him legally if he didn't want to be a part of it…either he was going to be in all the way or out all the way. My final note to him was defining his rights. It's amazing what one can educate themselves about in a week's time. I let him know that if he did not change his mind within the next six months, which was the duration of my pregnancy at the time, that when the baby was born, his name would not go anywhere on the birth certificate and it will have my last name. "Yeah, that's how I want it to be," he agreed. Before he got all happy about his decision, I told him to wait because I wanted him to be fully aware of what that meant. I further explained that after that moment, he will have limited to no rights. If at any time he felt regret and wanted to be involved, it would then be up to me to decide if he has anything to do with my baby. I told him that if life was going great for me and my baby or even if by the grace of God there was another man in my life, I would protect the best interests of my child.

My dad said I was being too nice by letting him know all that, but I wanted, as I stated before, to be able to be above reproach if there ever came a time in the future where this may need referencing to. If he ever comes back in the future or if my baby asks about his father, I want to be able to say I was straight up and honest about everything, having some peace knowing that I did what I could. At the end of the conversation, he actually had the audacity to ask me to "unfriend" his friends on Facebook, afraid that they would somehow find out or figure it out. I told him that I was letting him off the hook really easily already and that I would decide. I explained that if they asked, I could've just alluded to the fact that the father decided not to be involved, and if they had asked him, he could just say no. When it was all said and done, I did decide to cut ties with the mutual friends we had. He wanted it to just all go away, and why would I want to risk friends pressuring him into something he clearly didn't want? In that moment, I also knew that he hadn't told a single soul about me being pregnant…not friends, not family, not even his parents. Unfortunately, it's a burden, a secret, he will have to carry by himself until he ever decides to be free.

One thing I will never forget from this last conversation I had with him was the moment he started to give me his "woe is me" speech, saying how he told himself this would never happen to him. *Are you kidding me?* I let loose on him. "Do you think that after twenty-five years of being a virgin, I was super phyched about this? I "colored" outside the lines for the first time in my life and only after three months I got pregnant. Then do you know how hard it was to tell my family, more than half of which still thought I was a virgin?...and not only that I'm pregnant, but I'm not even with the guy anymore. And do you understand how hard it was to tell you, knowing already that in our hypothetical conversation you would abort it? It's not as if I didn't have plans either, but it's not like we're sixteen in high school. We're young adults who decided to take the risk." I actually did tell him all that.

During my pregnancy, the hardest part about his rejection was this lingering attitude I had towards him. Even though I was glad he had made his decision and a decisive one at that, I still had to deal with the anger and pain. I knew that I should have been furious about his rejection of my baby and his responsibility, but I was still burning over the break up. It took me a while to realize why, and this is the conclusion I came to: I was still upset because I don't think he realized how special of a circumstance our relationship was…how special I thought he was…how special I thought we were together…how rare it was. Knowing how amazing I am, I think I was just offended that he didn't find me or us the same. I was insulted. I WAS INSULTED. It seemed to be so easy to him. Breaking my heart was so easy. That's where my rage came from, feeling like I was just another girl when he was special to me…when I loved him. Thank God I didn't feel enraged all the time. I promised myself I would not become a bitter, cynical woman. But I have to admit that I never, ever, thought this would be in my story and eventually part of my future husband's story. This is my story now. It pains me to say it, but I would cry about that. It seems maybe selfish for me to think that way, but I can still remember the days when I use to pray for my future husband. How I would pray for his strength in life and relationship with God, and it killed me that now I would have to come to him with what seemed to be something a little less, not the way I imagined. Surely there was no way I could've seen this one coming, being pregnant and unwed at twenty-five. So when I would think about how light-heartedly my ex took our relationship after I had already told him about how serious and rare it was for me to even have a boyfriend, it would just consume me with rage. It was like I wanted him to feel how much it tore through my heart. Needless to say, I haven't heard from or spoken to him since that day.

The reality started to set in. This was happening. I, Jasmine Henderson, was now going to be a single mother. Things were never going to be the same, not in life and definitely not between my baby's father and I. I remember having several sobering moments especially within the first month.

I particularly felt the reality of the challenges my baby would face without a father when I happened to watch the movie "Courageous" randomly on T.V. As it turned out, it of course wasn't random at all that I ended up watching a film about Christian officers who were challenging themselves in fatherhood, realizing that the main ingredient it takes is courage. I was balling at every turn. I cried when one officer went to his father's grave and forgave him for abandoning him and again when that same officer had an intimate, vulnerable dinner with his daughter where he told her that she deserved a man who was not just going to win her heart but treasure it. But nothing hit home like the scene where one of the younger officers who had left a young woman from college pregnant and had never been there or seen his little girl in four years decided to change his ways. He wrote the mom a letter and sent her a check asking for forgiveness and a second chance. *Could I do that? Could I forgive him and give him a second chance after everything that had passed and after everything that would pass?* Again, I became frustrated about my situation.

One day as I was lying on my parent's couch, I truly felt the Grand Canyon-size rift between myself and my ex. I was listening to the cars driving by when suddenly I heard a car pull up. A dreadful thought came over me. For whatever reason, I got this feeling that it was him coming to talk to me. My eyes closed as my heart started to race. I imagined him walking up to the house, and I ran to meet him outside. My first thought was, "You can't be here!" It was out of rage but more for his safety that I yelled out. I thought of all my family and friends who wanted to literally fight him and beat him up. My eyes opened, and I realized the sound was just part of a daydream. I took a deep breath, a sigh of relief, and I closed my eyes again only to see his face and the moment that we shared when I thought he loved me…a moment that seemed perfect. This memory was of us at the park after his soccer game. It had seemed as though everyone had slipped away, and it was just he and I sitting there with his head resting on my lap, looking up at me with those eyes. I then opened my own again coming back to the present moment. *It will never be the same.* Sometimes I feel as though maybe I made it all up since he so easily gave me up in the first place…it's possibly more comforting to feel that way. How he could end it so coldly and turn his back on his child I may never understand. But one thing remains; it will never be the same.

This was all reality that I was facing, but there was also one lie that I began to tell myself. As much as I wanted a husband and a family, I began to tell myself that I was unworthy of it. *Who's going to want me now? I'm a "complicated" situation…a baby mama.* The record played over and over again in my mind, "You are unworthy." It had already been in rotation for years, but where the thoughts picked up momentum were after another movie I saw.

During a ladies night, we all wanted to watch the movie "What to Expect When Your Expecting" as kind of a joke since I was pregnant. The movie was really funny, but in following all the journeys of the different women, one theme was constant. No matter what crazy tangent happened or fight or whatever, in the end, the guys were there for the women and their babies. It was something I was not ready to see. Even the movie was saying that the men are supposed to be there, and here I was…alone. *What was wrong with me?…What was wrong with me?*

As things were settling in, I told a few more people in my close circle of family and friends. With most of my guy friends, they wanted to physically confront him and "handle" the situation. I'm not gonna lie, I knew it was bad when the younger of my two older brothers told me that my baby's dad better stay away from the house for a while. My brother has never been confrontational or violent in his entire life, but I could feel the genuine anger he felt toward him. He wouldn't have to worry about him coming over though. In telling my aunts and uncles on both sides, the general reaction was shock, disbelief, and love, but the last of my family to tell was the hardest. And that was my aunt and uncle from Missouri.

As a kid, I use to fly out to Missouri for about two weeks every summer. It was like a second home, and I honestly looked at them as if they were another set of parents. Yet again, theirs were more disappointed looks that I didn't want to face. As God would have it, they were flying out to Los Angeles a few weeks after I had found out, and I was going to tell them face to face instead of over a phone.

It was the last day of their trip when I mustered up the courage to tell them. We had a great time at the beach and hit traffic of course on the way home. In the traffic, I seized the opportunity, and the lump was thrown back down my throat. I could feel their heart break as tears came to their eyes when I told them. My aunt had worked at a pregnancy clinic before, and it was a close subject to her heart. We were all crying as I explained what happened and that my baby's dad knew but was choosing to be out of my baby's life. Like the rest of my beautiful family, I felt understanding, forgiveness, support, and love. One thing I got to explain to them was how I had gotten to the point of choosing to let go of my promise to stay abstinent. And that was a question I got to explore in the duration of my pregnancy. How did I get here?

A BROKEN VOW

4 HOW DID I GET HERE?

I have to admit that for a while, I was angry with God. Actually, forget saying I was just angry; I was pissed. I felt singled out and betrayed. I felt like the consequence for my actions were unfair. I had asked God for forgiveness, and I knew that He forgave me right away. But I was still feeling this disconnect…this distance from Him that I couldn't explain and couldn't seem to get past. I was praying, I was singing, I was going to church regularly. It seemed as though none of that mattered. It wasn't getting me any closer. Finally during one service, I exploded.

I remember the lesson being about how we turn from God and He continues to be there and give us the opportunity to turn back to Him. I mean, for anybody that should sound pretty amazing, right? But it was explained in such a way as to say that failure was inevitable and that it was our job to acknowledge, confess, and turn from it. Still, standard stuff, and don't get me wrong, I whole heartily agree. But I sat there in the pew, pissed, because I had deep wounds resurface with such tenacious vigor that it couldn't be ignored. I was angry and frustrated. What was God playing at? Because, it seemed like every time I found myself fervently committed a-new to God, something always seemed to come up and crush my resolve. I came to realize that I needed to share, out loud, what was going on and how I felt.

That day after church while we were eating lunch, I shared my frustration with my parents. I was so glad that I did. In turn, my dad shared his testimony with me about losing his job and the unjustness he felt at the time, explaining how it was the biggest blow God could ever give to him as a man. It's funny because that's exactly how I felt. I felt like if I would ever even consider turning my back on God, it would have been because of something like this. To be honest, the thought never crossed my mind. Instead, my circumstances simply drew me closer to Him. Still, marriage and family were my biggest dreams. It's not like I won't ever have those things, but I wanted to be a virgin and share not only that moment with my husband but also share my pregnancy with a man who loved me. My dad's vulnerability and honesty in sharing his story was the shift I was looking for to begin to repair my relationship with God. As I began on my quest of being a Godly woman and parent, I came across this chapter in the Psalms.

Psalm 25:

"A Plea for Deliverance and Forgiveness

A Psalm of David.

To You, O Lord, I lift up my soul.

2 O my God, I trust in You;

Let me not be ashamed;

Let not my enemies triumph over me.

3 Indeed, let no one who waits on You be ashamed;

Let those be ashamed who deal treacherously without cause.

4 Show me Your ways, O Lord;

Teach me Your paths.

5 Lead me in Your truth and teach me,

For You are the God of my salvation;

On You I wait all the day.

6 Remember, O Lord, Your tender mercies and Your lovingkindnesses,

For they are from of old.

7 Do not remember the sins of my youth, nor my transgressions;

According to Your mercy remember me,

For Your goodness' sake, O Lord.

8 Good and upright is the Lord;

Therefore He teaches sinners in the way.

9 The humble He guides in justice,

And the humble He teaches His way.

10 All the paths of the Lord are mercy and truth,

To such as keep His covenant and His testimonies.

11 For Your name's sake, O Lord,

Pardon my iniquity, for it is great.

A BROKEN VOW

12 Who is the man that fears the Lord?

Him shall He teach in the way He chooses.

13 He himself shall dwell in prosperity,

And his descendants shall inherit the earth.

14 The secret of the Lord is with those who fear Him,

And He will show them His covenant.

15 My eyes are ever toward the Lord,

For He shall pluck my feet out of the net.

16 Turn Yourself to me, and have mercy on me,

For I am desolate and afflicted.

17 The troubles of my heart have enlarged;

Bring me out of my distresses!

18 Look on my affliction and my pain,

And forgive all my sins.

19 Consider my enemies, for they are many;

And they hate me with cruel hatred.

20 Keep my soul, and deliver me;

Let me not be ashamed, for I put my trust in You.

21 Let integrity and uprightness preserve me,

For I wait for You.

22 Redeem Israel, O God,

Out of all their troubles"

When I read this passage, my heart was broken and then began to heal. I found myself so close to the end of my rope that I just had to let go and let God take over.

Later on in my pregnancy, I went to a women's' conference with a handful of co-workers, and it was there in those classes and testimonies that I really began to discover how far gone my self-worth was. It was also there in that weekend that my decision to recommit myself to purity was strengthened and confirmed. The weekend was about identity…our identity as women of God.

My discovery about my lack of self-worth started at the conference, but taking full ownership in my decisions and how I got there took a few months even after I had my baby. In piecing it together, this is what I uncovered:

I had made my decision long ago, ever since I can remember, that I was going to wait to have sex until I was married. I made my decision not solely based on my religious beliefs, but also based on all I kept learning about the risk of catching diseases, the risk of pregnancy, and the risk of a broken heart. To me, no amount of pleasure or sense of normalcy was worth the risk. I also fell in love with the idea of only having one mate, one partner, one love…that "two would become one." I knew what God had to say on the matter, but I also clearly remember a small voice that questioned, even at the very first declaration, if I was going to succeed or not. To think I wouldn't make it seemed absolutely absurd and impossible in that moment when I was so young, but you see, just as God had a plan for purity in my life, Satan had a plan for destructiveness. Right from the beginning he saw where he could get a foot in the door, and I remember gathering books on sexual purity and on dating to assist me and keep me strong. So how did I break a promise I had faithfully kept for twenty-five years? Satan's plan is patient, and I found that it didn't happen just all of a sudden. When I look back, I had set myself up to fail, chipping away at my promise piece by piece.

So my train was on the track of waiting until marriage to have sex, and rejection was the start of being derailed. Standing strong in my decision was easy in the beginning. Honestly, high school was a breeze for me. I would tell any guy I dated where I stood about having sex. I had a boyfriend as I was graduating who understood and supported me. Then when I went off to college, I dated and dated and dated and dated. I would choose these guys that really weren't on the same page as me, but I would expect and hope that they would understand. I set myself up to be rejected over and over or to reject them, mostly over the issue of sex. Each time a dating relationship never turned into a committed relationship, it would send a jolt right through my cars.

It didn't help when I would fill my head with romantic novels, movies, and family stories that would heap more coals into an already unstable caboose. I didn't tempt myself by watching porn or reading racy novels. My pitfall was watching and reading the exact opposite...stories about love. Every story I heard about, read, or watched, only caused me to be aware and long for what I was missing. Sex is meant to be an expression of love. Yes, I wanted to have sex, but more importantly, I wanted to have love.

In my pursuit of happiness and love, I started to slowly give up my boundaries. I would passionately make out, spend the night, dance close and seductively, all in the hopes of engaging a guy. I was also expressing something that is natural and healthy but is only meant for my husband. The crazy part was that the more I would hook up with guys, the less firmly my boundaries stood, the less meaningful whatever the physical touch would mean, and the less I was satisfied. They were all the physical expressions of love but with the absence of it.

Then came the conversation in my head that set me off to make one of the most important decisions of my life. I was twenty-five, and I looked around. I felt like the last virgin my age in Los Angeles. I noticed at the time that almost all my peers had made the choice to be sexually active despite having been taught the same beliefs. More importantly, I knew that my parents not only had sex but had two of us kids out of wedlock. Most of my family got married when they were young, and here I was twenty-five and not even close to being married. I had built up so much frustration by every rejection. The last straw was a guy I was talking to long distance for a while. For the first time in my dating life, I had put every thought aside about what the "man of my dreams" would look like and really focused on the heart…focused on his heart for God. I stepped out of my box and off my list. Through many deep conversations, I felt connected, and finally, when the opportunity came, I flew out to visit him. Long story short, it was a disaster. I ran into some of the same problems not of sex but of commitment that ended up with me telling myself the same lie. I'm too complicated for any guy.

All my life I've been told that I'm too intimidating for guys. In high school, I was a girl that knew what she wanted and had an opinion. High school guys weren't ready for that. Because of that, I began to hide myself. I began to leave out different parts of me that I thought a certain guy may not like or understand. I began to show the incomplete me. This totally backfired whenever I found myself being vulnerable with a guy, sharing every bit of my personality and character, and he would reject me. I've had a couple of guys say they wanted to be with me or even marry me, but their excuse was always that they weren't ready, that I had it "together" and they didn't. And in my mind, that translated as I wasn't worth the risk.

A few months after that experience, that was it! I was tired and frustrated with the whole thing. I felt as if God had betrayed me. *I've done everything You've asked of me. I've led a good life…a pretty faithful life. Can't I catch a break? I've tried everything, and still I'm alone. You're the one who gave me this natural desire, so why haven't You sent me someone already? Women use to get married in their teens. I mean, our period starts when we're about 11 or 12. This is cruel. If You're not going to handle this then I will.* Out of anger and resentment, I decided to do what I wanted. It was my choice anyways right?

Off went my train, derailed and skidding on the ground. I had sex. At the time, I didn't even care that I had broken my promise. I was so far gone. I chose to believe the lie. I was so angry that I didn't even care that I threw away something I had been keeping for twenty-five years. I disconnected myself. I felt like I was owed something. I had done what I was supposed to all my life.

I had sex with my baby's father before we even became committed to one another. In the beginning, it didn't matter if I loved him or not. I was having fun and having my way. It was only after we had dated for two weeks when he asked me to be his girlfriend that I had realized how irresponsible I had been and what a risk I had been taking. By the time we were broken up, I had come to love him, and a month later, I found out I was pregnant. Not only had I suffered the broken heart I was always warned about but also the pregnancy as well.

About a week after finding out I was pregnant, I had the opportunity to sleep with someone else. *What were the risks now?* And in that moment, I made the decision I still hold on to today. I decided to clean up the wreckage and set myself back on track for waiting to have sex until I am married. I've had friends and family members try to push birth-control at me and advice just in case I slip up or change my mind. But the thing is, I am aware of what led me to break my promise to myself and to God and am the wiser for it. It's never all of a sudden. That moment is a buildup of moments and events past.

A BROKEN VOW

5 PEOPLE'S JUDGMENT AND GOD'S FORGIVENESS

People, people, people. I know that we've come a long way from "the old days" where girls were shipped off to some remote place or religious compound to hide the "shame and disgrace" of getting pregnant out of wedlock and have made strides from the days of when they made people marry. But I'm sorry to say that as far as we've come, the church still has a ways to go in loving as Jesus loved.

For this reason, my pregnancy was kept under wraps at work for a while until I really started to show, which was at about six months. You see, the school that I was working for was the Christian school my grandparents had founded. It was bad enough that I could hear it in my secular friends' voices when I would tell them I was pregnant. "Oh, so you got married?" they would ask because they already knew where I stood. I was only having sex if I was married. But now, I would hear the judgment from some of the people who were Christians, and no voice rang louder than that of the new pastor of the church/school.

When it was finally revealed that I was pregnant to the staff, about a week later, I was pulled into my sister's, the director's, office. At this time, all the women of the staff had been very supportive and completely loving. I thought that the chat was going to be about another project she had for me. My position during that summer was P.E. teacher, after school programmer and teacher, newsletter writer and editor, Facebook page manager, and chapel leader for the Bible adventures curriculum. And in gearing up for the fall, I was preparing material for a parenting class my grandma and I were going to be teaching. We taught it together the year before, and now, on the verge of becoming a parent, this opportunity fit so perfectly. So with, as I said, all the different hats I would wear and with all the different duties, I was not expecting the following conversation. Basically, I was told that the decision made by the new pastor was that I couldn't do any of those things any more. I was restricted to newsletter and Facebook, which, according to my sister, I was lucky to even have kept my job. I guess I can thank the courts for that one, since apparently there are laws that say I couldn't be fired for being pregnant. He wanted to fire me.

I was filled with anger and outrage. "So he wants me to hide?!" I forcefully questioned. I know she was doing her best to try to smooth over the situation, but I had already had issues with this pastor before. My mind and my heart felt like it was exploding. My mom walked in the middle of the conversation. I kept raging, "He doesn't know, no one knows, what any other teacher or staff member does when they leave work. Just because you can literally see the consequences for my actions doesn't make anyone better than me or holier." When she hit me with the blow of not being able to teach the parenting class that coming fall, it was the last straw. I had been working diligently that entire summer reading books, watching DVDs, and typing up the book that we were going to use. My grandma and I had decided to take two different parenting books and make our own lessons out of them. It wasn't just saying goodbye to all the work, but as a future mom, I had really prayed about the topics and had seen the benefits already of the lessons I was learning. Now, I wasn't going to be able to bless some other parent who may really have needed to hear it and learn simply because they couldn't have someone like me representing the school and the church. The consolation apparently was that I could come back and teach it in the spring. "OK, so when my baby bump is gone and when I can hide my child, that's when I can come back. And what's going to change then? My heart will still be the same. The only thing that will be different is my physical appearance. If that's the case, I won't come back to teach here ever again." The passionate words just flew out of my mouth. I may have been a bit dramatic, and I slightly blame it on the hormones. But I felt it true. If I was unworthy then, in my eyes, I would be unworthy the rest of my unwed, single-mother life. My mom told me not to say that…that I didn't know where God was going to lead, so I should never say never. I can still feel the passion of my decision fill my cheeks with color. It took until my son was ten months old before I was able to "clear my name" and was granted an audience to see if I was "fit" to teach again. But at the time, I was about to quit right there on the spot.

Thankfully, that day we had an Earthdust session. Earthdust is an event called by the director to help the staff have a moment of just worship and prayer with God. Music is played for inspiration while the teachers go in shifts to sit in the sanctuary…and it was my turn. The music played and I cried and cried. I grabbed a piece of paper and pencil from the pew, and in that moment, this is what I wrote:

"My God Can"
My God loved me before I was even born
My God loved me knowing that I would run from Him
My God loved me amidst my sin
My God loves me even though you may not

You can't love me past my sins I have committed before
But My God can
You can't forgive me for what I have already changed
But My God can
You can't support me as a new creation
But My God can
You can't see past the darkness of my sin
But My God can

My God can love me unconditionally
My God can comfort me always
My God can give me another chance

My God's arms are always open

This is My God: The Creator of the heavens and earth
This is My God: The Author of the beginning and the end
This is My God: The Savior of the world
This is My God: The Example for all
This is My God: The God of my for-fathers

This is My God: The Lover of my soul

So there I was. I had cried my heart out in frustration, confusion, and was seemingly at the edge of my limit. I never thought I'd feel such judgment in the place I grew up in, the place my grandparents treasured, the place I had called home. By the end of Earthdust, I was strongly considering quitting. My sister came in the sanctuary and gave me a hug. It was Friday, and I told her I would take the weekend to think it over. It wasn't just about the injustice that I felt was being done to me, but how can I support a pastor who thinks and acts this way? Through much anger, I decided in the end to continue to work there. To be honest, I couldn't afford not to work. Looking back on it, I realized that my mom was right. Was I going to let one man stop me from fulfilling whatever God had planned for me? Who is man? I discovered that whatever his thoughts are of me, even to this day, it doesn't even matter. I can truly say that I have forgiven him for his judgment and prejudice. When it comes down to it, he'll be the one who will have to pay for it in his life, and I pray not for revenge but for his heart to be changed.

Unfortunately, his initial reaction and condemnation was only the beginning of 'wrongs' that were done to me, all of which were behind my back and never to my face. I've forgiven him now, but at the time, I felt acute injustice. What made matters worse was the thought that my ex didn't have to deal with any of this. The truth is, of course, he deals with a different burden, but I had to walk around with the physical evidence of what happened every single day. And I would deal with the feeling of wanting to quit almost every week. What could have been a purely happy and joyous time was met instead with hardship and controversy and even judgment and offenses by my own family.

I was appalled to hear that my other brother had said that I should have gotten an abortion. It angered me, but where he was at in his life and in his walk with God was a foreign, distant place. His words were only out of his own insecurities, coldness, selfishness, and lack of sense of responsibility he was facing in matters of his own son. Still, I wanted to strangle him because his son, my nephew, is the best thing my brother ever had the privilege to create.

Another account with my family was when I was explaining the injustice of the work situation to two other family members. They basically had sided with the pastor with one of them saying that this was a consequence for my actions. As if it's not enough that I'd have the "consequences" for the rest of my life as a single parent. I loved my baby, and it was going to be a blessing. But I was going to have challenges for the rest of my life. They tried to make the distinction of the title I would have after I gave birth, but I didn't and still can't see a difference. It made me feel as if I was wearing a scarlet letter.

Thank God it was only a small amount of people who were willing and ready to judge. The truth is there is no one righteous, not even one. God had forgiven me, and that's what mattered most. It would be a journey to forgive myself. I sought council with a pastor at a new church we were becoming members of. He was so loving and open. I felt my faith some-what restored in man again. I felt the love of Jesus shining through because there was no one "beneath" Jesus that He didn't love. Because, in fact, we all are beneath Jesus, and yet still receive His love and forgiveness.

And to whoever might be reading this, it is important to me that you know that there is nothing beyond God's forgiveness; there are only limits on forgiving yourself. God is loving and merciful and gracious. He will not stop you from reaping whatever you sewed. He is a just God. If you sew in sin, that is what you will reap, but the best part is that He will always love you. God does work <u>all</u> things together for your good as a believer. If you have not accepted Him as your Lord and Savior or have turned your back on Him, get right with Him today! Whatever you did or didn't do doesn't matter to Him and never will. He sees you and loves you for who He created you to be. God is not a man that He should lie, and He says He will never leave you nor forsake you…no matter the sin, no matter the crime, no matter the most hideous thing you can think of. Whatever you did, whatever you've done or thought about doing, if it is against God, it is not who you really are. You are a new creation, covered by

Jesus Christ, not just in some things but in all things. His love is unconditional and true and the only one worth living for. Don't be afraid to reveal yourself to Him. Revealing yourself isn't for God. He knows already. The reveal is for you. We don't even have to be afraid to approach the Father; He is waiting with open arms. He <u>always</u> forgives and can redeem any situation.

This is why going through this was the hardest thing for me to do up to this point in my life. Not only because getting married and having a family was and still is the biggest dream of my life, but because of the reaction I got through this toughest reality. If we are sons and daughters of God and are to be a reflection of Him, why did I not receive love, compassion, and forgiveness all around? Why did it take so long for me to forgive myself?...Their stings lasted for a season, but my judgments upon myself would prove to be harder to shake.

JASMINE HENDERSON

6 FINDING MY PEARLS

My mom told me once while I was venting to her about all the troubles I was having with dating, "Don't cast your pearls before swine." In the moment it seemed to make perfect sense. I knew my worth. Why would I date a slime ball? When my mom told me this, I was still pretty inexperienced in the dating game, maybe even just out of high school. Later on, I would find the challenge was this: OK, so who were the swine? I'm not saying that men are pigs or that all the men who disappointed me were swine, but if I were honest with myself, most of the guys I dated were undeserving. When I think about the verse, pigs don't even know what to do with pearls. So, we weren't even on the same level...different people. Also, I knew we were unequally yoked. They may have referenced their Christianity and/or faith, but I knew it was a gamble whether or not they truly believed, let alone if they were even ready to lead a household. Not only were they perhaps not my equal spiritually but also, I am awesome. I hid my greatness to match their level of mediocrity. My standards got lower and lower, and here's the amazing thing. <u>I chose</u>

<u>who I dated</u>. I didn't have to date any of them. But with every guy I dated, I gave him my pearls to weigh the value of them. At the level the guys were, who were they to value me? Forget the swine, what man at all has the right to tell me my value? Only God can.

So, what am I worth?

Unfortunately, it took this experience for me to even realize and admit how low my self-esteem had actually gotten. I was a strong, independent, secure, self-loving and proud woman for so long that it was truly shocking to find out that the way I was living was only a shell of what was really me. My self-confidence became only a facade. I had cast my pearls out for men to judge them, and rejection after rejection, I slowly buried who I truly am. So by the time I met my son's father, he seemed to be a breath of fresh air, and I ended up making exceptions for things I normally never would have. I hate to say it, but I was a bit desperate. I was so hungry to be wanted, appreciated, understood, loved. And it wasn't just the exception of having a sexually active relationship. I over-looked some of the staples and considerations that were on my "list" of important things because I felt that I could risk them for love, but I'm learning now that love, while it may feel like the sensation of falling or abandoning and running towards something amazing, is also centered and grounded in everything I've ever wanted…fitting perfectly. At that point of my life, I was living in the "why not?" state-of-mind, but I now realize that it's so empowering to live with the realization and ownership that I get to create and choose whatever and whomever I want in my life, not just settle with whatever is showing itself at the moment.

Well, I already told you how I had gotten to my low point where I broke my vow. After throwing my pearls in the heaping mud pile with the pigs, I got to take hold of them once again, clean them off, and proudly wear them.

Owning up to the fact that I was only a mere shell of the confident woman I am was the beginning. I saw my poor pearls in the mud and rescued them. Oh, the mud! There was so much crap and gew not only from dating experiences but experiences in general. You're in denial if you say that life hasn't affected you in some way. We simply breathe and life throws stuff at us. Experiences can seem to be good or bad, either way, through them it can reveal things about ourselves or can cause us to make up certain beliefs about something, someone, or group of people. What's crazy is I'd been throwing my pearls for people to tell me if they were valuable almost all my life. Twenty some odd years of a habit is hard to break. It wasn't until I started to re-discover my value that I realized my pearls were never to be judged by any man or woman. It didn't matter what they thought at all. In fact, even saying I was "rejected" is a matter of interpretation. All they did was say no. It wasn't personal. Either way, whether people like me or not, I know who I am…I know who's I am. You think I'm amazing…I don't care. You think I'm terrible…I don't care. I'm amazingly wonderful no matter what. God has made me in His perfect image. I am a part of what He looks like, what He stepped back to look at after creating and said that it was good.

My first bit of healing and reconnection to this epiphany

happened when I went to the women's conference I mentioned before. As I said, I went while I was pregnant. It was put on by Shepherd of the Hills: The Vine, and the theme was Arise. It was my opportunity to begin shedding things from the past and grab hold to the creation God's made me to be. The person Satan would love to keep me from recognizing. There were shadows that were cast throughout life to keep me in the darkness, but I am a brilliant light. I am beautiful. You are beautiful. YOU ARE BEAUTIFUL. I sang this to God the first night there. "You make beautiful things/ You makes beautiful things out of dust/ You make beautiful things/ You make beautiful things out of us." Through the retreat, I was reunited with ideas of who I am and discovered new definitions of who I was called to be as a woman. It was an amazing start. But to truly live every day as this beautiful powerhouse of a woman that God created me to be, I would go through another journey of revelation and transformation.

As I mentioned before, in the beginning of my pregnancy, I saw the movie, "Courageous." From that moment on, I knew that I wanted to be a courageous woman, the best woman, I could be for my baby. I was on a mission to do whatever it would take to be an upstanding and powerful woman of God. And just like God, He brought something so amazing I couldn't have asked for anything more perfect. A friend of mine brought me to a training called M.I.T.T., Mastery In Transformational Training, and in five days, it rocked my world in the best of ways, letting go of so many things in the past and stepping into the authentic version of myself. It was so freeing to return to being the Jasmine I was as a kid, and with that, learning to live my life with her ways of being while handling adult responsibilities. It was like I took the fast track of cleansing myself, forgiving myself and others, and taking my power back. A few pearls I cleaned off through the process and rediscovered were: my voice, self-worth, beauty, trust, vulnerability, intimacy, abundance, commitment, availability, womanhood, independence and dependence on God, and power.

I am a courageous woman! I feel as if I am running the race now on purpose, with purpose. I am unstoppable. I say this again, it is never too late for God to restore you, but it starts with being aware and acknowledging the past because Satan will keep it replaying in the back of your mind and choose how you live your future. But once you are aware of it, then it takes the courage to choose something different, and therein lies the power. God did not create us to be crippled but whole. He is our kinsman redeemer, our advocate for reclaiming what was thought to be lost, and now that I've retrieve and washed off my pearls, I plan to keep them adorned upon my neck for all to see and never give them away again.

JASMINE HENDERSON

7 MY TRUTH ABOUT SEX AND A NEW RESOLVE

There is no mystery what mainstream society has to say about sex. For most of you, you deal with it on a daily basis, bombarded by messages that encourage casual sex and multiple partners. And most of the time, casual sex is flaunted and praised without presenting many of the possible repercussions of such risky ventures. We all know what the possible risks are such as viruses, disease, pregnancy, and even emotional damage, but for me, it's not enough to focus on why I shouldn't have sex but why I'm waiting.

Sex is beautiful. It is fun and pleasurable. In the Bible it is described as a moment when two become one, when a woman and a man leave their families to cleave to one another to begin something new. God created sex. He made it to be enjoyable, but I believe He also created it to bind a man and woman…a physical act that is emotionally binding. Is it possible to have sex with "no strings attached," no emotional ties? Some people think they can compartmentalize sex, but even if there is no emotional response to the person, I believe there still is a response to oneself. I still gave a piece of myself away. And knowing what there is to gain by having sex with someone that you truly love and trust, why pretend it's not worth waiting for…why instead make it casual? If sex weren't so complicated, it wouldn't be so beautiful. I mean, God knew how much we would enjoy it. He gave us the drive. But when the box is opened, whether it was done in love or not, that drive demands more and more, and without true love at the center, it's just a physical act. One movie asked, "Why can't sex just be like playing tennis?" I think the real question is why would you want it to be?

When I was still a virgin, I remember a lot of friends, mainly guy friends, asking me questions like, "Wouldn't you want to make sure that you were compatible in bed? What if he/it sucks? What about his size? Wouldn't you want experience?" I told them then, and even after everything I've gone through, I still believe it now more than ever. God will take care of me. Imagine that. Granted, most of the friends who asked me this weren't Christian, but how come I can ask God to take care of everything else but not my future mate? How can I trust that everything in my life is a good and perfect gift from God, and yet worry about sex compatibility with my future husband? Also, as if we won't have years to work on it and perfect it? Those other questions are selfish in my opinion, all about serving and satisfying self, not to mention entertaining the pattern of always looking for something better, something new and different. The grass is always greener on the other side right? Is it that phenomenal to believe that the man I believe is my soul mate will also be perfect for me in sex?

And then they would ask, "Well, what if you wait all this time, get married, have sex, and then get divorced? Then what?" I want to tell you, that is their fear, and if it's yours as well, again, whom do you trust? I tell you the truth that God is worthy of our absolute trust, and if you have doubts, tell Him about it! It's not as if He won't already know. Do you have concerns? Tell Him or talk to an upstanding, Christian friend or mentor. Notice I said a "Christian" friend. Be careful who you go to for counsel and advice.

Not only do I believe that God created sex to tie us together in a physical and emotional way but also to procreate future generations. **If you are not ready to have a kid of your own, you should not be having sex.** More than the physical or emotional damage, I'm choosing to be abstinent because I couldn't stand the possibility of doing to another child what is now the story of my son. I'm not saying that every guy is going to abandon his responsibilities or that God can't redeem a situation, but this is the risk I am most unwilling to take ever again. My son is now being raised by a single mother and may never know his real father. I've settled that guilt with God and myself, but I'm telling you, I wish I never even had to deal with it in the first place. For the rest of my life, I will get to navigate this road, figuring out what's best for my son and what's best for me. My son is an absolute blessing and by far one of the best things I've had the privilege to create. I want the best for him, and that's what I want for the rest of my children...the best.

This is what drives me now. This is why it is so important that I get this message to you and to the world. The future of the world begins at the home, and right now, our homes are broken. They are restorable, but they are mostly broken. Men and women of this day and age are selfish, in my eyes, to choose themselves instead of their future, their legacy. And what will you choose to leave behind? Who will you choose to be for your children and their children's children? Sex is way bigger than you, bigger than the immediate carnal pleasure. How many more broken homes need to rise up, how many more baby killing abortions have to be performed, how many more orphanages and foster homes need to be created, how many more neglected and passed around children have to suffer before we realize that it's not just about us…not just about what feels good in the moment? Sex is bigger than you.

God has called us to something greater. You can look at God/Christianity having the view of abstinence as an overbearing rule that means God/Christians just aren't any fun, or you can see it as a helpful piece of advice that actually makes sense. God doesn't want us to not have fun. Remember, He created sex and created fun. He wants what's best for us, for our spouse, and what's best for our family and future.

If you are sexually active right now, it's never too late to change the game and for God to forgive you and restore you. If you are a virgin, I pray that you have chosen abstinence until marriage and continue on that path, being aware that there will be challenges ahead but God will always be there to support you. If you're married, I hope that this is something you can share with your kids now or someday, and I also pray that you share your own story. If you are a fellow single parent, my request is that you not stay silent about your story, forgive yourself, and know that God can and will restore your family and make it whole.

No matter what your response is to my story and message, I only ask that you begin to have this conversation, that is so important and pivotal, within yourself and your community. I pray that in candidly sharing my journey, it has given you the opportunity to discover something within yourself and, more importantly, discover something about our amazing God.

WHAT'S YOUR STORY: STARTING THE CONVERSATION

The purpose of sharing my story is for the community to start having open and honest conversations about sex. Our society, whether Christian or not, needs to have these talks. Sex not only affects our lives but the lives of our families…our future. In my opinion, it is also a huge and important subject matter that is barely and rarely touched upon in the Christian world.

If you are doing this as a group discussion (which I pray you are), I encourage you to do the following:

1. Open with prayer
• Please allow God to be present in your discussion.
2. Set a safe space
• In order for people to swim out into the emotional trenches and go deep, they gotta know that there won't be storms of judgment that will drown them.
• What is said in this space stays in this space.

3. Be honest

• Sometimes confessing or admitting thoughts, actions, or feelings is the first step to healing and understanding.

4. Love and Forgive Yourself

• In my experience, you cannot truly love until you love yourself. Also, you cannot truly live freely until you free yourself.

5. Pray for one another

• There is a battle going on. Imagine fighting with a whole army instead of by yourself…winning seems possible and the battles not so scary.

Conversation Starters:

1. Finish this sentence. To me, sex means…

2. How do you really feel about abstinence? Is it…

   a. realistic/possible

   b. something best left in fairytales

   c. the only way to go

   d. an "old-school" ideal that has no more relevance

3. Did you or do you talk to your parents about sex? Why or why not?

4. For me, my family's history of getting married at a young age affected my decision to have sex. How much does or did your family's history affect your decision?

   a. Not at all

   b. Very little

   c. Yes, I consider it

   d. I think about it all the time

5. God created sex. What are some things that you talk or could talk to Him about?

6. If you are a parent or were to become one, what kind of "protection" talk would you give to your child?

   a. Condoms

   b. The pill

   c. Abstinence

   d. I don't even wanna think about it!

7. What kind of talk did you get from your parents? What kind of talk would you have wanted?

8. What boundaries or rules have you set for a person that you're dating or when you were dating? Do they or did they work?

9. Shows like "Sex In the City" and movies like "The Brothers" cast serial dating with casual or even monogamous sex as something to be normal, celebrated, and admired while showing commitment as something to be feared…something not to be trusted. I believe this idea leaves many people choosing to be single until they are at least in their early to mid-thirties. How do you feel about that idea?

10. I know that I have become the best version of myself after becoming a mom, and I feel blessed to have the opportunity to build my life around my motherhood and my career. Does/did the thought of marriage or parenthood before your life is/was "ready" scare you?

11. What are the qualities you want in your partner?

12. What do you want sex to be?
   a.   When I'm in an exclusive relationship
   b.   Whenever I want it
   c.   When I'm with my husband/wife
   d.   I never want to deal with it

How will that affect your life and relationships?

13. Whether you're choosing to have casual sex, monogamous sex, or sex on your wedding night, nothing is guaranteed. How can you trust in God when it comes to sex?

14. Studies have shown that there is literally a bond that is created with sex after an orgasm. The release of the hormone, oxytocin, creates that bond, and the more you have sex with that person, the greater the bond becomes. Even your body points to an idea that sex

is meant to bond one to another...two becoming one. Do you believe that a person gives a piece of themselves away again and again by having casual sex? If so, would you want to?

15. A) For those that are having sex out of wedlock, do you feel like you are more in control ("owning your man/woman-hood") or drowning (trying to find yourself)? How is that working for you?

B) For those that are abstinent, have you been tempted with the life of sex before marriage? Do you feel out of control or trust Who's in control? How is that working for you?

16. As I mentioned before, it's not enough to think about all the negative reasons to be abstinent. What are some positive reasons to wait?

17. If you could create a "dream" family for yourself, what would it look like?

18. Have you come from a broken home or one that's still together? How has that affected your view on family and relationships?

19. The National Fatherhood Initiative has posted research done by the U.S. Census Bureau stating that there are 24 million children, one out of three kids, that deal with biological absentee fathers from the home. Do you think that sex out of wedlock affects this statistic?

20. Jesus started his ministry in his early thirties and was never married. Being in a man's body, do you think that He may already know some of the struggles of abstinence?

Again, these are simply ideas to get you started. And whether you're married or not, sexually active or not, sex is relevant. It is important to talk about. I pray this is only the beginning of a beautiful conversation. Thank you for being a part of my journey and my own conversation. May God bless and keep you.

JASMINE HENDERSON

NOTES:

ABOUT THE AUTHOR

Jasmine Henderson is on a mission to discover and reveal the many beautiful colors that paint the masterpiece called woman. The perfect helper by design and created purposefully different than man, woman is the completion of creation in her glorious feminine grace and strength. Jasmine's ministry is geared toward uniting this powerful force – WOMAN.

Born and raised in Los Angeles in an inter-racial home, Jasmine has an eclectic perspective and background and has seen the importance of impeccable role models. She was brought up in a Christian home and environment and became a believer at a very young age. With teaching in her blood, she has naturally fallen into that role coaching soccer for various clubs, academies, and schools and leading Bible studies and praise and worship.

By playing soccer in college and professionally, Jasmine has been able to see a good portion of the world, and just as she has seen the power of soccer unite and bond countries together, she prays that her ministry will do the same to unite Christians and women all over the world.

Jasmine is looking forward to the many adventures God has planned for her and her son.

Made in the USA
San Bernardino, CA
14 January 2014